FALSE CREEK

FALSE CREEK

JANE MUNRO

**HARBOUR
PUBLISHING**

1 2 3 4 5 — 26 25 24 23 22

Harbour Publishing Co. Ltd.
P.O. Box 219, Madeira Park, BC, VON 2H0
www.harbourpublishing.com

Edited by Jan Zwicky
Cover image courtesy of the artist, Ranjan Sen
Cover design by Anna Comfort O'Keeffe
Text design by Carleton Wilson
Printed and bound in Canada
Printed on 100% recycled paper

Supported by the Province of British Columbia

Harbour Publishing acknowledges the support of the Canada Council for the Arts, the Government of Canada, and the Province of British Columbia through the BC Arts Council.

LIBRARY AND ARCHIVES CANADA CATALOGUING IN PUBLICATION

Title: False Creek / Jane Munro.
Names: Munro, Jane (Patricia Jane Southwell), author.
Description: Poems.
Identifiers: Canadiana (print) 20220242941 | Canadiana (ebook) 20220242976 | ISBN 9781990776090 (softcover) | ISBN 9781990776106 (EPUB)
Classification: LCC PS8576.U574 F35 2022 | DDC C811/.54—dc23

for

Andrew, Justin, Julien, Ella, and Will

TABLE OF CONTENTS

THE TONGUE, THE PENIS, THE BRAIN

THE GOLDEN BOAT

and lapilli – burning pumice stones
rain down on Pompeii and
mudslides bury Herculaneum

Pluto seizes Proserpine not for six months
but for two millennia – the rape
can be dated

24th August CE 79

but what I do not understand is the depth
of soil covering homes, villages, cities
erased without a volcanic eruption

beneath Anatolia's rolling grassland
excavations uncover
Lydian, Greek, Roman layers

earth must fatten as it ages

I understand how forests
prairies, canyons, steppes, marshes
rise, fall, compost, build duff and humus

the fungal kingdom decomposes
remains of plant and animal kingdoms
middens of clamshells pile up by villages

but – how fast those villages – cities – empires – disappear

garbage tips, landfills
the trash we toss gets buried by more trash
and digested by mycelium

earth shifts
lifts ranges, rearranges
tectonic plates

ice melts, oceans overflow, Vancouver may wash away

FALSE CREEK

WALKING HOME FROM VANIER PARK

that evening, I didn't know I'd arrived

walked right over the site where the longhouse sat
I didn't know

it had been home to 15,000
before the onslaught of European diseases

that evening in a Bard on the Beach tent
with the city as backdrop
watching a performance of *King Lear*
covering my eyes
when Gloucester's are pried out
weeping
with Edgar, weeping with Gloucester, weeping
with the Fool, with Lear
weeping with Kent, and almost unbearable
Lear carrying Cordelia, laying her out
showing Kent the tremble of a feather
Break now, heart
weeping

with Poor Tom
in the storm – Lear's mirror – shedding
identity, protection, sanity, all
save the Fool's kindness

walking home late
uphill

coming back to look

into blackberry thickets
trash tips
walk overgrown rail tracks

cross under Burrard Bridge
study the shoreline's rip-rap bank
below lawns

strolling Canada Geese
city archives
planetarium, Maritime Museum

I can't even find
the stump of a giant fir
coming back

to look
and maybe…see
it's hard to see

hard to believe
I didn't know
I didn't notice

WHAT COUNTS AS VIOLENCE?

a poster on a toilet door
explains verbal abuse is violence

when a doctor asks
is he violent
I hesitate – what does he count
as violence

inattention
to pick up a party favour
from a neighbour's placemat
slip on the wrong pair of flipflops

ignorance
to settle on land the crown allotted
buy property with a registered title
believe it's mine

my family's racism
an aunt justified by saying
for their own good
red birds don't marry blue birds

how about assuming I'm not at fault
when my country's government rips children
from their families, communities, cultures
traps them in residential schools

starves, sickens, abuses
and kills them
erases names, murders languages
hides facts: this was not *terra nullius*

to face truth
as its beneficiary, I commit systemic violence
shame
feels violent … does that count

HOW COME THIS CRUELTY?

215 pairs of children's shoes
on monumental steps
to the closed back door
of what was Vancouver's courthouse and jail
now is the Vancouver Art Gallery
across from ice rink
university
law courts
above two blocks of underground parking
430 shoes in Tamara Bell's installation

sea to sea to sea
the underground parking of children

persons pacing with radar to map erased graves
rain on grass around structures

Onward Christian soldiers
in white dogma, coif, veil
dog-collar
blinkered senses
women below men
children below women
foot soldiers
marching as to war

sea to sea to sea
dominion

domination
children out of place

O Canada we stand on guard for thee
on a ceiling in the Vatican
at the top of the Great Chain of Being
God reaches out from a brain packed with angels
to connect with man
empires lay train tracks
newcomers stake claims, break land
take lives, grow wealth, power plants
punish to train
true patriot love in all thy sons command

below children
shoes

graves sodded over
to see ... to see ... to see ...

what is this war

ERASING

maps
names given by newcomers
Vancouver, the Lions, False Creek

conceptions
my mother held
Canada: a just and caring country

mottos
UBC's *tuum est* – it is yours
it is up to you

erasing
the goodness
of my family

these are erasers
    a block of soft art gum
    the firm thumb of a pink rubber
    nubs in metal collars on the ends of pencils
    a gritty ink eraser that scrubs a hole in paper
    stinky white-out
    felt blackboard brushes
    that girls take outside and clap
    together after class

those erasers don't wipe out
ignorance

no simple overwrite corrects assumptions
woven of memories
on a loom of belief
how to use a knife and fork
be a man
dress
protect oneself and one's family

SUNSET BEACH

I am alone
at the mouth of False Creek
though the beach sand is trampled
and couples lie on towels by bikes
sailboats, paddleboards, kayaks go by

and across the water on the planetarium
signs say: This building is closed
due to COVID-19
ditto on this side for the Aquatic Centre
where I took swimming lessons
my kids supervised in a playroom
and afterwards, holding the baby, the four of us
splashing and laughing
in the saltwater wading pool

now
at "the place inside the head of False Creek"
the Skwxwú7mesh Nation has approved
the development of six thousand new homes
in eleven towers
on their eleven-point-seven-acre reserve
at the south end of Burrard Bridge

it will have
seven hundred parking spaces – bike-sharing
its own power
at least seventy percent rental housing
this is not a city decision but
Vancouver will have
a new hub

when my grandparents
moved to Vancouver from Newcastle
and lived on English Bay, women
paddled across to sell
berries and fish, and baskets
made of tightly coiled cedar roots and grasses
decorated with cherry bark

that was before 1913
when the BC government
forced them onto barges
burned their homes
ousted them from the city
deposited them on the North Shore

this history
was not related to me
though I grew up here

ignorant – insensitive
to these and other truths
about my country's values

now
on this sunny April afternoon
snow receding on Mount Elphinstone
named by a British surveyor
after a Scottish peer and naval officer

freighters
wait at anchor in English Bay
Spanish Banks in the distance
Point Grey topped by UBC

I don't know the names
for these mountains, promontories, shores
islands and inlets
trees, berries, mushrooms, seaweeds
fish, birds, animals
with whom they lived
moon after moon
season after season, for thousands of years

the blue mountains, blue sea, blue sky
today
look as they looked
long before
newcomers named this shore
Sunset Beach

FALSE CREEK

chock-full

    not with dog walkers – photographers – buskers
    cement trucks – rowing sculls

    tubby little ferries
    zigzagging shore to shore

    piles of mangosteens – tuna fillets on ice
    buckets of star-gazer lilies

    no painted piano for the public to play
    no stack of yellow wheelbarrows for marina members

populated

    with eel grass – sea asparagus - bladderwrack - bull kelp
    oysters – clams – mussels – abalone – crab - octopus

    surf smelts – oolichan – herring spawn
    chitons – sea urchins – periwinkle – moon snails

    humpback whales – sturgeon – sockeye – pink – coho
    canvasback – goldeneye – bufflehead – dunlin

    great blue herons – hummingbirds – bald eagles
    kingfishers – ravens – waxwings – owls – sandpipers

    martens – porcupines – salamanders
    wolves – frogs – elk – bear – otter

dogwood – bitter cherry – elderberry – bunchberry
thimbleberry – blackberry – huckleberry – salmonberry

skunk cabbage – monkey flower – devil's club – bleeding hearts
ocean spray – nodding onion – camas

mutated

native wetlands
"water coming up from ground beneath"

eastern two-fifths of the inlet, its estuaries
and tidal flats, filled with refuse and rubble

sand bar at the western end
buried by an up-dredged island

False Creek four fifths filled in
now one-fifth its former size

haunted

by a 1,350 year-old Douglas fir
a 1,835 year-old yellow cedar

by lichens – mosses – ferns – soap berry – wild roses
canoes

languages I don't know
spirits I can't see

retained

by mountains – still blue – behind Yaletown
an abused body of water – inlet to the heart of Vancouver

Main Street, near False Creek's
"hole-in-the-bottom"

listen, love

overnight, the tide dropped again
the seawall's masonry
neatly fitted

look at this

two turtles soak up sun
also neatly fitted
one to one

in bulrushes at the edge of a pond

he's got slides of me in his basement
with dark, dark hair
a carton of slides

running water has dark, dark hair

this is where
dredges dumped sludge
sawdust burned

layered currents

booms of logs
turned into studs
into siding

listen, love – have you got

a sifter
a lemon
a stockpot

you, across the hall

dark, dark hours
skin in ripples
we are water running – running out

love, listen – listen, love

A BODY OF WATER

is alive
tides
an inlet's breath

currents embrace
barnacles, mussels, oysters
cobbles, gravel, granite
support
kayaks, fish boats, yachts

carry alder leaves
dusty with pollen

its skin
antic with wind
and the orbits of raindrops
welcoming
moon trails

reflections of sunrise

buried
it leaves ribs, femurs
many metatarsals
its skull and winged hips
in the rubble above it

not that water
appears
armatured

by anything calcified
but a body's ghost
might take surprising forms
if only in
a city's imagination

and strata do layer
clam shells and otter trails

if awareness resides
atomically – in atoms
and speaks
elementally
quick steps with generations

of steam, cloud, droplet

whiff of moisture
sappy trickle leaves to roots in phloem
water bearing minerals lifted by xylem
if awareness is found
underground on Mars

if water is alive
body out of body out of body

COMING OUT OF CHOICES

IN THE PARKING LOT

coming out of Choices with four litres
of milk – there – huge and pale
you, moon
just risen in a still blue sky

you can't wait

I must change – lose
my hide
something we haven't seen before
is coming

THE BOY I'M NOT

is shrouded in indigo
blue veil windowing his face
as in a burka
he is smaller than me

sitting side by side, we look
like one draped person with two heads

I marvel at our inky hair, moon faces
he is as old as me, just recessive
he widens me
this is the body's kindness

indigo reminder of persons uncounted
voiceless persons

lingering as the soul
grows its capacious banyan
a city's watershed beneath our homes
and in ourselves, a forest

why indigo
because it's naturally translucent

as any evening sky
because like woad
it's fermented from plants
because it's old

MOVING WATER DOES NOT HOLD

the leaf it carries
moon
now gibbous – swollen as a pregnant belly
flows from phase to phase

my hand goes
to where your heel jutted up
hello, you
passing through

and yet, you are you
another discrete body
earth and moon
pas de deux

a few golden birch leaves cling
to the tips
of slender branches
snow

flakes fall – it will snow
all morning the forecast says
and in three days
the moon will be full

its face gliding
horizon to horizon
when I see you, moon, scale cloud drifts
yes, it's you – light on your feet

NURSING THE MOON

small, frail, not a good latch
not tugging on the breast
not sucking milk out

the hours it will take to fill
this new moon – make
that much light

days the nipple falls out
milk spills, unswallowed
you pass the moon across, attach it

to your other ache
distended
your blouse drenched

warm belly's sour smell
the moon
can't take it all

stops gaining
starts to shrink – you can't let it go
cannot bear no light

asteroid – another one, deflected
millions between Mars and Jupiter

T-Rex down the drain
waking with sleep dust in my eyes

a jet of ghost particles aimed at us
blazar – the gulping
remote emitter of neutrinos
endlessly passing through masses

and space in a straight line
undeflected from perfect balance

between plus and minus, left and right
energy and matter, latent and ambient

from a black hole
to Antarctica

found, but can we stop
the ice cap from melting

time on a bicycle with a bell
ding, ding, ding coming up behind

me on the sea wall – another rising tide
I fear Steveston, all the delta lands, sunk

the river laid down long mud flats
most days, way out into the strait, a plume of brown

comet's tail – streak in a cloud chamber
plump alpha particle, electron's wispy zigzag

on my back on an island beyond light pollution
shooting stars mid-August

what I see is a massive plank
in an unfinished wall
held in place by poles and lashings
people slip it in
above other long thick planks

in Egypt, the New Kingdom collapses
Babylon declines, Mycenean writing disappears
Aryans settle on the Ganges plain
Hebrew tribes unite under Saul
Celtic migrations begin

here, people weave baskets from cedar
water-tight, finely twined
in my dream, the baskets remind me
what Europeans named the New World
was Old

MAP TIME

Exhibit at Vancouver's Museum of Anthropology, 2019
Marking the Infinite: Contemporary Women Artists from Aboriginal Australia

to map a walk … dots
a branch tip dipped in paint
makes on a tablecloth-sized canvas

her steps, her mother's
the story's steps
those she's allowed to repeat

their great salt lake
salty wanderings

of feet … whose articulated bones
we're born with
that grow … hidden … inside skin

grow calluses thick on heels
step by step
to be borne

on a walk at the pace our soles step
step, step … wade … double back

along the marge
to map footfalls … dots
to map a soul: does a city

have one
original
prescription

does an inlet
to map a river: the whir

as wheels
turn, turn, turn on pavement
background sound of traffic flow

as calluses are grated off soles
by women who don't speak
much English

in narrow shops
subtitles on screens for reality tv

appointment, appointment
to get
there on time, finish on time

their memorized phrases
and chatter in Vietnamese
currents of a busy street

other passages
pre-historic…up-river, down-river

coast sunk
under a mile of ice
bedrock scoured slowly, glacial erratics

long river swung brown into ocean
lays down
its delta's growth spurt

to map time
from which vanishing point

before salmon
before ink
before genus *Homo*

walked out of Africa
or our planet coalesced
if that's what it did

to map the ephemeral, mark the infinite
where we're at … what's beyond us

women use sticks
and patience
think blooms, fruit, a few colours

to mark a fleet of footsteps
to map … to keep
to leave … dots

MACKAY CREEK

I cleared a shelf close to its flow
left hemlock cones, smoothed stones

heard the water's poem
without knowing
as water knows

swayed on vine maple trunks
arched over pools and rapids

felt safe in a place where I had nothing
to achieve, no one to please
the creek withheld nothing from me

BELOW MY HORIZON

I can't see it but already
the moon is full

it will rise at 9:38 pm
and shine through my windows

I'll go out to the park
to see this Sturgeon Moon

big and white and mottled
as the fish who used to swim

in False Creek
August's full moon – full city

rooms bleached with reflected light
stars – a few of which I'll see

is there memory
in the chemical, magnetic, chronological

discernment of tides, crystals, roots, a virus
is light – our universe – a reflection

A LADDER

horizontal bars, vertical supports
tight intersections

a ladder
holds your weight

climb step by step
at your own pace

it wouldn't be a ladder
if it were just a pole

it wouldn't be a ladder
if there were only cross pieces

ladders on ladders reach rooftops
or well bottoms

sailors go up and down rope ladders
on a swaying mast

we mount to new thresholds on dilemmas
we retreat on relentless paradoxes

even when we're afraid to move
it's safe to go up or down

to reach a different point of view
from where we've been

mistakes and failures are parts
of an athlete's practice

DECISIONS MUST BE MADE

it's a sunny morning
we are in the kitchen

while away
I incarnated as a tiger
a Bengal tiger, big and beautiful

a journalist has arrived
she follows us into the bedroom

will the tiger sleep
on the top bunk
as myself, I sleep on the bottom

dual beings – dual forms of one person
the journalist comes with us to a restaurant

the tiger is seated at our table
acquaintances are at adjacent tables
one asks me, why are you all over my dreams

I reply
I want to talk with you, but not now

everyone smiles
we are going to a concert
the tiger has my ticket but so do I

the problem is
I've died – that is why I was away

they are left with everything
what will they do with my notebooks
dying was a mistake

my unease is a warning
decisions must be made

the journalist asks how
did the tiger happen
the answer is simple: I wanted

to be a tiger
big, beautiful

it's no zanier than a particle
splitting when fired through dual slits at a screen
daft as a dream, but deft in passing

an alligator
curled like a dropped cape
around the legs
of a chair
at a party on a lawn

the guests don't see it

its eyes bulge
as it lunges

I jump back
yank my arm
out of my jacket

the alligator
rips off
the jacket's sleeve
it almost got
my right hand

to lose my dominance

blindsided
could I learn to write

chop – stir – dress – unlock doors
drive stick shift – use a mouse
with the hand that was left

sing blues
harmonica, slide guitar
from the sunken lands
for a hand
no one would hold

MOON BOAT

still floating high
but flushed red

twenty-two million in Cairo

on the mountain top
where couples go to do their stuff

the wind so rusty
we can't see the Great Pyramid of Giza

streams of red taillights
on matchbox cars

the frog in my throat

the dust of Cairo
in King Tut's time

fewer than two million
humans on this globe

earth's moon boat
sails across the sky

heeled over, on a fast tack

THE TONGUE, THE PENIS, THE BRAIN

sheathing our bodies
the obesity of words
about our species

soothing for a baby

not transfigured
by its gist
but I wish I knew Mandarin

Arabic, Bengali – understood

the language spoken by spirits
composted beneath me
who slip into dream, raise goosebumps

the arousal of resonance

we explore its ferment
find more moons around Jupiter
calculate the composition of stars

plant chips in brains

to mesh machines with thought
so an artist with Parkinson's
can make collages, talk, and walk

we grow neurons in test tubes

plough continents of knowing
witty with organisms
oblivious to our racket

we note a red giant

tuck in its constellation
nighty-night
with a mind-blowing cosmic smack

THE TONGUE, THE PENIS, THE BRAIN

do not have bones
nor do the eyes

but it's bones that last

skeleton on a hanger in a classroom
left when a book is closed

in your hands, the weight of bone

what is left of a father
when you wash his armature

where to inter love

to embody another
not as a mother does an unborn infant
to embody
one not you, say – a god

how would it feel
to have four arms
what muscles would spread
your back, strengthen

shoulders and neck
when you throw and hold and do
with four hands
how would your brain

coordinate
twice the dexterity
twenty fingers
or – simply be a man

deciding how best
to spend your time
how to meet their needs and yours
would it be clear

which of your priorities
might shift
could you play act being
Vishnu, Shiva, Ganesh

or just – a man
a healthy, capable, kindly
man
living your life

it is easy to forget
which did up the coat lined with leather
wind could not blow through
snugged the waistband of bell bottoms
secured passport, visa, pen
the knife with folding tools
glasses case, car keys

to forget for years which were
the unused spares
for the rose cardigan
mother knit painstakingly
and I lost
in grade one, after school
playing on a far-away street

it is not impossible to lose
every button on every shirt I ironed
the smoothed feel
when doing them up
top button open
quick kiss
it is easy to forget

which did up the heart
snugged the groin
closed the eyelids
a shortbread tin of closures
a corridor with doors
some locked, some not
a long corridor: more and more doors

EACH KERNEL'S BEARD GLISTENS

plush crop wind strokes
just to brush air's skin on sun's promise

polishing green almost to silver
before yielding the wealth lifted from soil

the rippling abs of the continent

quaking aspen take over
abandoned trails in a bush my friend tended

what's happened to the paintbrush
that filled the ditches – where are the daylilies

cabbage moths flirt when the wind drops

canola – no longer called rapeseed – candy bright
bison a gourmet meat – stock markets, Roundup

acres of wheat just before sunset not yet golden
but glorious, light to be kneaded into loaves

what makes the fields vibrant is their under standing

of green beneath the grain's shining heads, glimpses
of stems, leaves – an under story of shades

soil built up over decades of farming – centuries
of grasslands, herds of buffalo, people who followed them

walking with shades, I seek shade to walk in

THE RENTAL COST OF SUPERIORITY

a rifle, hidden, glints

rabbits in the grass
eat baby carrots from the hand
of a girl whose heart is melting

this year's thousand leaves

on an elm
harsh winters saved
from bark beetles and fungus

roaches

dandelions, viruses, mycelium
will survive when humans
don't

a prairie

green with too much rain
sloughs no longer show a white grin
bulrushes host fewer warblers

stars – where earth's been and is going

a fullness we roll close to
when it comes as a cat
creeping into a dream and we sigh

let grief go

surprising how comforting
the approach and departure of sheet
lightning – hail

how remarkably small the foundations

of what was a two-storey house
olive stove in its rubble
gaping oven

angels

their ladders
and summer trapeze artist acts
in the big dome

atoms

connected
disconnected – one fine cucumber
picked from its vine

COME INTO MY ROOM

In memory of Father James Gray, OSB
And his genius for friendship

as you did that morning
greet me with a bear hug
scold me for my disarray

weeds on your grave thicker now
and mowed, leaves on the elm
flicker outside my window

no hand-written letter
no card falling out: *Shekhinah!*
if only we knew our glorious partner

dread slows and chills me
come into my room
friend with your intuition

as if you abide here still
even if you've fled
to Ursa Major

black bear in your black robe
pad down the hallway
smell my disarray

the tenderness
of witness – to hold what is unbearable
to bear it

BANNER IN ROME ON A MUSEUM

solitude is to the soul
what food is to the body

emperors closed the passes
during the winter solstice

in the solitude of snow
trees freighted

in the wilderness of a city
the manna of solitude

soul, you can be as lively
as the wind

INEXTINGUISHABLE

fire pit in the Beach House
ashes on smoothed pebbles

ocean paces, not to itself a start or finish
I, who am to myself neither parent nor progeny

wait for tidings
to turn and return me

the ball in my hands
a clew of thin, blue ribbon

wrapped around charm after charm
until, at its centre, a silver heart locket

and then there comes you
the light who goes in it

SWIFT AS A PEBBLE SKIPPING WAVES

bounding ridge to ridge
the terrifying hound is down
needle teeth pierce my palm
volcanic eyes

call the police

her face tells me – they'll shoot it

it won't let go

but then, like pulling a sock
inside out to hold its mate

the volcano is a painting a friend made
the teeth are a shark's
    seized by an osprey
    airborne and thrashing
the dog is the one
settled on my feet
the ridges are on islands
    a coast of ridges, inlets, islands

we each have a glass of Sauvignon Blanc

she's cooking
we talk

this too is a dream

Sarah Cooper is lip-syncing

the future is under construction
and potentially dangerous

raw plywood walls screen
No Frills' checkout

and interior from the street
I look through a plywood corridor

at its far end a shadowy stream
of figures pass

counterclockwise, one by one, some with carts
no detail, no substance, to them

it's not clear
where or how to enter the store

no windows with bananas promise
No Frills won't be undersold

I smell the plywood – it reminds me
of my father, what he built

how I wasn't with him
when he checked out

so much yearning in that mixed bag
of what he bought

they say
the primordial snake, Adi Shesha
    is the bed of Vishnu
    the Hindu deity
    sustaining the universe

as the gut carries us
those ancients imagined
    our entrails
    reflect an original macrocosm
    in our microcosm

coils
maintaining me
    incarnate
    a great serpent on whom may rest
    self-preservation

THE GOLDEN BOAT

TAKASHI MURAKAMI

Exhibit Vancouver Art Gallery, 2018
Kaikai Kiki Co. Ltd.

cement apartments cantilevered out
stacked high and higher
vaults above False Creek
above Granville Street bridge
above buses and six lanes of traffic
above eagles, seagulls, wind-blown walkers

catacombs under Alexandria
carved into limestone
spiral staircase
a well to radiating halls
leading to individual and family
burial chambers

preachers blaring from loudspeakers
their words criss-cross and collide
against buildings, echo
through narrow streets
lined with prayer mats
men and boys bow under the deluge

on a gallery wall, Murakami's
gold leaf background
embossed with skulls
and Murakami's
black background
embossed with skulls

Takashi Murakami hides skulls as well
as the dead are hidden in catacombs
and the flattened-to-their-screens-sad
are coffined during lockdown
in cement blocks
they do not walk beside False Creek

they do not meet
black bears, grouse, eat salal berries
paddle hand-crafted canoes
sleep under stars
they do not know the smell of their grandmother
could not track her

HIS HUGE CANVASSES

immediately make sense

you cannot comprehend
a book with one look

but his painting fills my peripheries
five minutes, ten

I step closer
see manifold details

as if through a telescope, I look
at light from earlier and earlier

Murakami employed

art assistants – 200 worked
24/7 to complete *The 500 Arhats*

to connect grieved victims
of tsunami, the meltdown of a nuclear power plant

to this grotesque, super flat explosion
of legendary enlightened Buddhist monks

Murakami's canvasses
an amusement park

opening first in sci-fi Doha

offer a hard-edged
measurable, predictable, controllable background

to reassure as it destroys
the glamour of idols and beliefs

creating bizarrely
ordered relationships

which, in a book's linear way
it may also embody

Haldane said, "The universe is not only queerer than we suppose,
but queerer than we can suppose."

To calculate quantum physics, mathematicians use imaginary numbers.
Turok said, "In a very real sense, we all live in an imaginary reality."

On my walk to the grocery store
I pass a yellow rose and carry its scent with me.

Then, the busy intersection. A couple – engaged in conversation
veer toward me. I sidestep.

As they pass, I realize – her Golden Retriever
is a service dog. She's blind.

All I'd noticed at first was that they did not notice me.
He was bearded. The dog, but neither of them, blonde.

Walking home, I pause to sniff the yellow rose.
Yellow with red smudges. Above a cluster of earlier stems, cut low.

At home, the bathroom mirror tells me I forgot,
preoccupied with Haldane, to wear my false front tooth. No implant yet.

Maybe the cashier wasn't looking. Or was being polite.
It's a bit bizarre – at core, even my false tooth is spacious and in motion.

despite social isolation, borders closed

as the sun rose, the glistening green back of an Anna's
leaf-size hummingbird on the feeder

after curfew – protesters
in Hong Kong, New York, Paris, L.A.
unmasked – phones high

ginger root, apple, cranberries, grapefruit, spinach – in a smoothy

how quick to find, then compost, moth webs
in the pumpkin seed jar
for three days, a kitchen without moths

I still do not understand why
desire departed – or, for that matter, desire arrived

what was not an adventure

an expectation the day was long enough
to get everything done, and the fact

or the size of the universe – inequities of birth – packing heat
or what loosens the suction cup holding up the bath brush
such a clatter in the tub

and what was

June gloom despite cottonwood fluff
in the grass on the margin of the path
a lanky fourteen-year-old looking down on his dad

good morning
in the shower, mind tingling already

how I am moved

by the curious courteous way
words convey what they don't say

the wonder of a conversation
six feet apart
·but present

CINNAMON CURLS

he with his arbutus limbs, waves
to her with semaphore flags
from the porch of a caboose
at the end of a train paused at her crossing

green, she sketched him at first
but then russet
firm and sleek, nearly slippery
to stroke

her house dizzy with drawings
papery strips curling – evocative, quick
satisfying as is the madrona in every season
racemes of bloom, evergreen leaves, berries galore

rooms sweated late summer
he signals – this train comes
your way again soon
we won't lose synchronicity

TO THE ARTIST'S DISMAY

at the opening
his mural
was not his mural
figures added, all in blue outline
all looking left
out of his masterpiece

a long wall
of mountains, inlets, valleys, islands
rivers, lakes, ocean

of beings
in every size, age, colour, species
their homes, bridges, towers, institutions
towns and cities, farms and docks, ships
and railways, highways, lighthouses
forests, scree slopes, meadows

the majesty
of what he'd painted
day and night

balanced on scaffolding
slaving over composition, perspective, harmony
he'd drafted, corrected, perfected
with intent, passion, decades of practice
study, perception, discernment
brushes, knives, rags – laid down

layers on layers
dollops of every shade, tone, tint
on his palette

now, subtly
his creation
not his work
and he doesn't know
how
this happened

the blue figures
woven into crowds, apparent in forests
profile after profile turned left
to draw the viewer's gaze
out of his picture
away from its focal points

at the opening, the artist
dumbfounded
to discover his homeland, life, inspiration
shameful
his beautiful wall
a display of what he did not see

cottages, cedars, yachts – even flatware, sterling
a desk, a democracy

you don't expect one to fail
no, it takes an axe to break one
a war, a mallet, a forest fire

sovereign after sovereign after sovereign seemed sure
to their peasants and nobilities, six Georges were sure
each shifty as oceans are shifty, but in his time glorious

our animal wariness seems sure
as a grandmother's recipe, a father's slide rule
your alarm at the error of a saw felling a street plum

when crustaceans migrated from their coral reef
our woodlouse ancestors harboured water
to film their gills and pond their offspring

eons later, a human, likely wide-awake, bore you
afloat at first, then breathing
terrestrial, you too

who laughed in the bathtub, took to walking then hiking
sailed Lightnings, questioned with aplomb
who could imagine your good news deemed fake

BALLAST

fiords, inlets, the fingers of gulfs
between us

tidal bore of pain flooding ashore

living aboard as he does
with his chemo

up and down

lunation after lunation
moon's gravity on the tides

again, *E. coli* counts high

this inlet fed nations
oolichans and gulls, otters, and eagles

now exhausted permafrost vents methane

heat dome slaughters
starfish, mussels, clams

despair…deep and deeper…the steady unbearable

False Creek
Vancouver's keel of grief

WITHIN AND WITHOUT

the north's Great Bear
dips low
into star marsh

tongues
the dark's berry shine
one peel

of a tiny fruit
coracle
on a river of time

an indigo bunting
transfixed as a hatchling
by Polaris

annually pilots
1,200 miles north – 1,200 miles south
on night flights

offshore
a harbour seal
steers by the polestar

and dung beetles
dark as the dark they travel through
navigate by the Milky Way

before sextant, before compass
wind, waves, and stars
tessellated

the geometry of human passage
on the open Pacific
island to island

bird, fish, current, constellation
a choir of natural signs
by which the outrigger found its way

SALUTATIONS TO THE EVER GENERATING ONE

A self that goes on changing is a self that goes on living.
Virginia Woolf

    the smidgen I see
    of our universe
           though suddenly I see that word
           uni-verse
           one stanza
  one room
  in a mansion
           but without a brain
           does a universe
           have choice
  without nerves
  or sense organs
           could it feel
           perceive change
           be conscious
  drinking bird
  needs water
           to feed
           the apparent perpetual motion
           of its illusion
  change
  not unbegotten
           water
           the surprise
           source of energy

fifth metatarsal on the right
I heard it snap
but I walked every day
in an air cast

sometimes around False Creek

to keep going
helped it heal
and kept me sane – or, as sane as possible
not stuck inside, out

and about amidst throngs

of notes – heartbeats, breaths – conversational
snippets – foment of atmosphere – passing – pacing
not with Poor Tom, alone with my own
Fool, good body, your kindness

False Creek in its fitted cast: can water be broken

not unless it freezes
evaporated, mist
scatters – undone, dispersed – airborne
water doesn't shatter

weeping, water flows

tears, raindrops, words, thoughts
small and almost invisible, one by one
morsels of bone grow into a gap to repair a fracture
braced by air, pressing but giving, in a boot

inlet which is also an outlet

BURY ME IN A BUTTERBOX

under an apple tree

return me to my mother
where I lived before breath

take me out of seasons and sensations
let me learn otherwise

when you sleep, feel my arms
light as light, my hands

dovetailed joints knit with yours at corners
sunshine is not diurnal

cream the curds of the universe
spread galaxies on your bread

cut the Spartan to find its star
seed your soil, plot after plot

THE GOLDEN BOAT

the golden boat
one hand's length – curved as a cupped palm

thin as Agamemnon's death mask
but not Greek – the golden Irish boat

from the 8th century
in a glass case not far from the River Livy

through whose mouth many fled
oppressor after oppressor

tiny oars, also of gold
spider's leg oars

a boat to carry prayers – how do prayers
row ceaselessly – across seas

green with drowned ancestors
drowned dreams, the haunt of griffins

a golden boat of perfect proportion
to hold a poet – a crew of poets

from a fabled land
who also row without cease

NOTES

p. 21   S̲kw̲x̲wú7mesh Nation: The name S̲kw̲x̲wú7mesh contains several
sounds that do not occur in English or French. It takes some prac-
tice, and face-to-face instruction, for an English or French speaker
to pronounce the name correctly. Without phonological training, it's
not possible to learn the sounds from a book. But for English speak-
ers, an approximation of the sound of the word is this: *skwuh-HOO-
oo-may-sh.*

p. 37   A blazar is an active galactic nucleus (a super-massive black hole in
the heart of a distant galaxy) with a jet composed of ionized matter
travelling at nearly the speed of light. The difference between a quasar
and a blazar is the angle of the stream. A blazar's jet streams directly
towards Earth, a quasar's jet streams at an oblique angle.

p. 40   *Marking the Infinite: Contemporary Women Artists from Aboriginal
Australia* was the first exhibition of all-women artists at the Univer-
sity of British Columbia's Museum of Anthropology. Nine women,
celebrated artists from remote regions of Australia, explored the
immutable tension between the universal and the specific and
the power of traditional Indigenous knowledge in an increasingly
digital world.

p. 50   The Great Pyramid of Giza (also known as the Pyramid of Khufu
or the Pyramid of Cheops) is the oldest and largest of the pyramids
bordering present-day Giza in Greater Cairo. It was completed
4,580 years ago and was originally 145 metres high. One of the Seven
Wonders of the Ancient World, it is a marvel of mathematics and
engineering.

p. 62   Shekhinah is the English transliteration of a Hebrew word meaning dwelling or settling and denotes the dwelling or settling of the divine presence. In some accounts Shekhinah appears as physical light.

p. 75   The quotation in the first stanza is from an essay by J.B.S. Haldane (1892–1964), "Possible Worlds", in *Possible Worlds and Other Essays*, (Chatto and Windus: London, 1927, p. 286). Haldane was a British scientist who worked in physiology, genetics, evolutionary biology, and mathematics.

   The quotation in the second stanza is from *The Universe Within: From Quantum to Cosmos*, by Neil Turok (House of Anansi Press, 2012, p. 95). Turok is a world-renowned physicist and a director emeritus of the Perimeter Institute for Theoretical Physics.

p. 85   The poem's epigraph is from "The Humane Art" (written in 1940) by Virginia Woolf (1882–1941) collected in a posthumous book, *The Death of the Moth, and Other Essays* (Hogarth Press, 1942, p. 44).

ACKNOWLEDGEMENTS

My gratitude goes to all who helped shape this book. Profound thanks to first readers of the entire manuscript, Roo Borson and Gayle Raphanel.

Thanks to Ian Williams for early comments and encouragement; Wendy Sarkissian for her enduring enthusiasm for my poetry; Adrienne Drobnies and others who listened with appreciation to readings; Mimi Gelman for her "Decolonial Aesthetics" course at Emily Carr University of Art + Design; Jay Powell, University of British Columbia anthropological linguist, for his guidance as I sought to learn more about Indigenous names; and Guy Immega for his videos of me reading some of these poems.

Thanks to Jan Conn, Mary di Michele, and Susan Gillis for our many years of friendship and collaborative practice composing renga as Yoko's Dogs.

Thank you to the wonderful folks at Harbour Publishing, including Anna Comfort O'Keeffe; Annie Boyar; Coralie Worsley; and Jan Zwicky, freelance editor for the manuscript.

As always, the love and kindness of my family keep me going. Thanks to my children and their spouses: Ian and Becky, Alison and Gordon, Ann and Mark; and to their children: Andrew, Justin, Julien, Ella, and Will; and to Jock.

ᴊᴀɴᴇ Mᴜɴʀᴏ is a Canadian poet, writer and educator. Her poetry collection *Blue Sonoma* (Brick Books, 2014) won the 2015 Griffin Poetry Prize. Munro's recent books include *Open Every Window: A Memoir* (Douglas & McIntyre, 2021) and the poetry collection *Glass Float* (Brick Books, 2020). She has taught creative writing at universities across British Columbia, led writing workshops, and has given readings around the world. She lives in Vancouver, ʙᴄ.